SWATI SENGUPTA is an author and former journalist. Her books include *Out of War* (Speaking Tiger Books, 2016), *Guns on My Red Earth* (Rupa, 2013), *Half the Field Is Mine* (Scholastic, 2014), *The Talking Bird* (Tulika Books, 2014) and *A Tea Garden Party* (Pratham Books, 2021). She translated *Murder in the City* (Speaking Tiger Books, 2018) from Bengali to English. Swati runs a workshop series on gender for young adults. She studied English at Jadavpur University and lives in Kolkata.

Also in the series by Swati Sengupta:

Jhalkari Bai: The Braveheart Warrior

Milkha Singh: The Runner Who Could Fly

Birsa Munda: The Great Revolutionary Leader

Savitribai Phule: The Fearless Reformer

Arati Saha: The Swimmer Who Wouldn't Give Up

Bhagat Singh: The Indomitable Freedom Fighter

Satyendranath Bose: A Great Scientist of the World

The Incredible Life of Anandibai Joshee

The Girl Who Fought to Be a Doctor

Swati Sengupta

Illustrations by
Devashish Verma

talking CUB
An Imprint of Speaking Tiger Books

TALKING CUB

Published by Speaking Tiger Books LLP

125A, Ground Floor, Shahpur Jat,

Near Asiad Village, New Delhi 110 049

First published in paperback in Talking Cub

by Speaking Tiger Books in 2024

ISBN: 978-93-5447-880-2

eISBN: 978-93-5447-839-0

10 9 8 7 6 5 4 3 2 1

Typeset in Georgia by Jojy Philip

Printed at HT Media Ltd, Greater Noida

For Swapan Kumar Chakravorty

and Bhaswati Chakravorty

Chapter One

Eight-year-old Yamuna was looking at herself in the mirror. The other girls had been making fun of her looks. Again. Yamuna looked closely into the mirror. Were they right? Was she really 'ugly', as they whispered? She didn't think so. In fact, what she saw was the image of a stunning young girl staring back at her. She was not fair complexioned like other Chitpavan Brahmin women, with their sharp noses and grey, green or blue eyes. True that *her* skin was dark and there were small scars on her face.

But when she looked closely, she saw her sharp and piercing eyes, her dark, long hair that fell on her face covering part of her large forehead. She was short and strong and she could beat her cousin brother in wrestling! Who had heard of a girl winning against an older boy? That's why she was also called *malla* (wrestler).

Yamuna ran outside, skipping and hopping through the winding corridors of her home. It was a large house though it was old and dilapidated. She sat on a broken wall engrossed in deep thoughts. Little Yamuna was convinced that her mother, Gangabai, did not love her, though Ganpatrao Joshi, her father, more than made up for it. He recognized her intelligence and strength and encouraged her to study, showing off her reading skills to jealous and angry neighbours and relatives.

At that moment, a sudden excruciating pain sliced her scalp. Gangabai was pulling her long, flowing hair. 'What are you doing here, sitting on the wall, swinging your legs like a man?' she barked.

Yamuna stayed quiet because she knew crying would only anger her mother even more. Gangabai dragged her down the corridor. Tears rolled down little Yamuna's eyes. Suddenly, Yamuna's grandmother appeared and snatched the stick that Gangabai was about to bring down on Yamuna's back. 'If you use that stick another time, it should fall on my body,' the old woman yelled at her daughter. Gangabai left the room in a huff.

Why does my mother never speak to me affectionately? Tears rolled down Yamuna's cheeks. Her grandmother cocooned her within her arms. 'Be strong,' she said. 'Soon, you'll be married and go far away, and then she can't beat you up anymore!' she consoled her granddaughter. She fetched a tall glass of hot milk and some nuts. 'Drink up,' she said, her eyes twinkling, 'and you'll be strong and beat anyone hands down!'

Yamuna smiled. Her mother's violent behaviour made her feel unloved and restless, but her grandmother's affectionate touch was like a soothing balm. Even then Yamuna knew she had a tough life ahead of her. She had to think of a way to make her life different from that of others. Something that would make her shine so brilliantly that they would all praise her.

Yamuna would find a way, though she did not know what it would be right then.

~

Yamuna lived in the town of Kalyan, 40 km from Bombay (now Mumbai). She was born on 31 March 1865, the fifth child of Ganpatrao Joshi and Gangabai. Ganpatrao had been married earlier but his wife died young, leaving behind a son. He then married Gangabai, and they had nine children. Four of them survived—three girls Kashi, Yamuna and Sundara, and one boy, Vinayak.

Ganpatrao Joshi had a soft corner for Yamuna, and as she grew, he began to think of ways to channelize her unbridled energy. 'Little Yamuna is bright. But she plays all day. If I can make her sit and study, she will stop her mischief,' he thought. But it was easier said than done. Few Indians in the nineteenth century thought about formally educating their girls, and even fewer sent them to schools. Ganpatrao decided to arrange for Yamuna's studies in one part of their house. This had a huge impact on Yamuna.

Whenever a relative dropped by, the proud father would send for her.

'Recite a poem!'

'Read out a few lines!'

'Show them how you write!' he would ask her, flaunting Yamuna before the visitors, who were now shell-shocked! Why teach a girl so much?

At this time, there were many debates going on about the education of women. Formal education for girls was not common. By the time Yamuna was born, Savitribai and Jyotirao Phule were working for the education of girls in Maharashtra, especially children of the shudras and ati-shudras. But the education of girls from the so-called upper castes was not common either. Progressive men keen on educating their daughters met with stiff opposition, as was the case with Ganpatrao. And even while he thought of educating her, he remained trapped by age-old practices like child marriage. Girls were supposed to be married very young.

When Yamuna turned eight, and still a groom could not be found for her, Ganpatrao got worried. He could not afford to pay a big dowry. After a lot of searching, a prospective groom was located nearby. Gopalrao Joshee, a widower, aged twenty-six, had joined as the postmaster of the nearby town of Thane.

'Widower and twenty-six!' Ganpatrao wondered, downcast. His daughter was less than nine! But he was well aware that he would have to settle for this match. Gopal Joshee agreed to marry eight-year-old Yamuna, but he had a condition.

'I want to educate the girl and there can be no interference from your side,' Gopal Joshee said.

A huge burden was lifted from Ganpatrao's

shoulders. 'What problem can I have regarding that! She shall be your responsibility,' he replied gleefully.

In 1874, when she was only nine, Yamuna was married to Gopalrao Joshee. The little bride Yamuna was re-christened Anandibai Gopalrao Joshee. Marriage was meant to be a new birth for women, and thus a new life began for little Anandi.

Gopalrao had taken up the task to educate Anandi, but he had absolutely no idea what a brilliant mind she had, and what glorious goals she would set before herself to achieve.

Chapter Two

Gopalrao Joshee was different from other men of the times. Was he eccentric? No doubt he believed in women's freedom and education. But he also held traditional beliefs. Gopalrao was born in an orthodox Brahmin family of Maharashtra. As he lived alone due to his transferrable job, Gopalrao moved to the Joshi household after marrying Anandibai.

When girls as young as six or seven used to be married, they continued to live with their parents and moved to the husband's home when they reached teenage. But since Anandi and Gopalrao lived in the same house, they were in close proximity. He also became her teacher. A complex relationship grew between Anandibai and Gopalrao. He wanted her to do well in studies and her education became almost an obsession for him. She, on the other hand, was young and obstinate. Due to this, there were frequent conflicts. And this showed in terrible ways.

Gopalrao would hit Anandi whenever she disobeyed. Once, he beat her up so mercilessly with a piece of wood that her back was swollen. He apologized to her, but that was not the last time he beat her up, nor the last time he said he was sorry for it.

Gopalrao and Anandibai's families were worried. Perhaps the tension between them was due to his obsession with her education. Both families grumbled about this unusual marriage.

'Don't you fear that an educated wife may begin to write letters and run away with another man?' someone asked him. Gopalrao snapped: 'If that's the case, I'll be happy to not carry her burden forever.'

Gopalrao was soon transferred to Alibag, south of Bombay, and Anandibai went with him. They made a home together, though her grandmother was there too, since the bride was a bit too young. However, it was a small home and there weren't many distractions. Here, Gopalrao found the ideal condition to educate his bride and young student, Mrs Anandibai Joshee.

Anandi also became a mother at this tender age. She was taken to her parents' home in

Kalyan. There, at the age of twelve—just a child herself—Anandi gave birth to a boy. She was thrilled to bits! The tiny life that she held in her hands looked like a doll that slept through most parts of the day. She was filled with wonder at how a little life could be nurtured and born out of her own body!

But even before she could cherish and feel the joy of motherhood, the child died within ten days. Anandi was shaken. 'It is due to lack of medical care that my child could not survive,' she told herself, tears rolling down her eyes.

She soon returned to Alibag and threw herself into her studies to deal with her sadness. Gopalrao was a strict taskmaster. If Anandibai made the slightest mistake, he would throw a fit. But Anandi kept quiet. She did not know any way to escape, so she bore it with courage. Inside, she made a resolve: 'I will tell him how much I hate being beaten up. But I can do it only if I become learned and earn the respect of others.'

Gopalrao was full of contradictions. While he was physically abusive towards her, he also showered Anandi with unusual forms of affection like taking her out for strolls around town. When he first suggested it, Anandi was shocked. Women did not go out on walks with their husbands! What would people think? But he liked doing the unthinkable, and it made her rethink established norms as well. When people saw them together, walking side by side on the streets, they had contempt in their eyes. They even spoke ill of the man for showing such 'progressive' attitude.

Gopalrao was frustrated. Life in Alibag was stifling. Perhaps some other city would have some broadminded people? Seeking escape, he asked for a transfer.

Their next destination was Kolhapur in Maharashtra. Thirteen-year-old Anandi moved with Gopalrao, seeking happiness with him in a new city. Anandibai enrolled in Government Female School here, though soon she had to discontinue school for some reason. Gopalrao continued to teach Anandi, but was looking for a woman teacher for her.

'So many hurdles are coming our way. Perhaps we could have moved outside India, to the United States,' Gopalrao thought. For many, this would be unthinkable, but Gopalrao was somewhat eccentric, very different in his ways of thinking.

No sooner than he thought about it that he began to seriously explore the possibilities.

How could one pursue studies in America?

How much would it cost?

Where would he get all the information?

He approached Reverend J.M. Goheen of the American Presbyterian Mission at Kolhapur with a proposal for them to move to the United States for Anandibai's education. Reverend Goheen was excited to learn that an ordinary Indian was keen on chasing such a dream. He asked Gopalrao to write to Reverend R.G. Wilder of Princeton, New Jersey. In September 1878, Gopalrao did so, detailing his plan. He explained his wish that Anandi would pursue higher studies, while he was keen on finding some employment. But Gopalrao and Anandibai were asked by Reverend Wilder to stay on in India and convert to Christianity. It was a disappointment that Gopalrao found hard to accept.

He became restless again. He could not face rejection. How unkindly they were being treated even by their own people because they were progressive! Which city would offer a good education to his wife?

It helped that his job was transferrable. This time, he applied for a position in Bombay. It worked. The Joshees moved to Bombay in 1879. Gopalrao was in charge of a post office in Girgaum. Things started on a promising note here. Anandibai was enrolled in a school run by the Society for the Propagation of the Gospel. It was close to their residential quarters and Anandibai was happy to go to this school. Things fell into a wonderful rhythm of home and school, lessons and cooking. But she was in for a shock when the lady in charge of the school asked her to read the Bible and threatened to expel her if she did not do so. Anandi returned home disturbed and vowed never to go back to the school.

Surprisingly, Gopalrao asked her to go back, and said that she would not 'lose anything by reading the Bible'. Though Anandi was taken aback, she understood the need to be tolerant and open towards the teachings of other religions.

Going to school was unusual for married Indian women of the time, and in doing so, Anandi had to face many nasty comments. Wherever she went people stared at her. She had to walk to school every day as she couldn't afford to travel in coaches. But seeing her in a saree with stockings and shoes and carrying books in her hand, aroused astonishment in everyone around her. Seeing her, many halted their carriages, some stopped in their tracks, while others laughed.

Shopkeepers would spit when she passed by, and some even dared to make indecent gestures at her. Anandi's skin crawled, her stomach churned. She was traumatised, but she kept moving knowing that some day these words and gestures would not hurt her. Sadly, this kind of reaction was not uncommon for the time towards women who stepped out of the home and tried to pursue an education. Savitribai Phule, too, faced people's wrath as she walked every day to teach in school.

Anandibai learnt to deal with the staring and the harsh comments. She enjoyed her studies and her new-found freedom.

Soon, another transfer, another destination beckoned. This time it was Bhuj, in Kutch. For the first time, Anandi moved outside Maharashtra. Here, no good school could be found, and Gopal taught Anandi Sanskrit. A tutor taught her English, sewing and knitting. After a year and a half, it was time to shift base again.

Chapter Three

In 1880, a sheer coincidence would change Anandibai Joshee's life forever. Thousands of miles from India, Mrs Theodocia Carpenter from Roselle, New Jersey, sat waiting at the chamber of a dentist in a town called Elizabeth. It was not far from her home and she was waiting to be called by the doctor, and leafing through magazines strewn across the desk.

Something caught her attention. The magazine was *The Missionary Review* of Princeton. In it was printed a correspondence between Gopal

Joshee of Kolhapur, India and Dr R.G. Wilder. The Indian, Mr Joshee, said that he was hopeful of taking his young wife for higher education to the United States of America.

Theodocia tried to imagine the face of a young Indian girl. What hopes she must be nurturing to travel to a far-off land to educate herself! Theodocia had two daughters herself, Eighmie and Helena. Before leaving the clinic, she memorized the address of Gopal Joshee from the magazine.

Back home, she was in a fix. Should she write to the unknown Indian or should she forget about it? Theodocia could not forget about the couple, the story of their dreams and aspirations, and especially the young girl. After a few days,

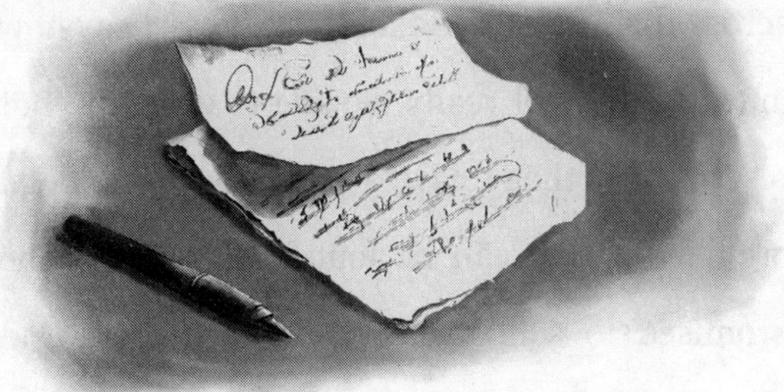

on 7 March 1880, Mrs Carpenter wrote to Anandibai Joshee:

Dear Sister,

I do indeed think of you as a sister, which is why I have addressed you thus. We are all children of the same God, and should therefore be ever ready to offer whatever help or encouragement we can to anyone born in a country less favourable to mental progress than ours...

Theodocia explained how she had come across their names and address. 'I can't say how much help I will really be able to give you, but rest assured that I have a strong desire to help, provided a way can be found,' she wrote. She promised to send Anandibai newspapers and magazines to provide her with information on American culture, customs and so on.

The letter from this unknown American woman moved the fifteen-year-old Anandibai to tears. Was this real? Could people actually be so kind as to write to strangers and offer help? Her own people had treated her so miserably.

Anandi replied to Theodocia.

Dear Madam,

So I address you as you are my well-wisher and far superior in intellect and learning. I am only fit to sit at your feet...

She told Theodocia how tough it was for her to pursue education in Bhuj. She had to study at home with the help of her husband. Anandi explained that she was 'anxious to study medicine and serve God and man thereby'. And so began a steady and frequent exchange of letters between Anandi and Theodocia—the beginning of an unusual, lifelong friendship and kinship. Each letter was filled with curiosity about the other's culture, daily life, religion and social practices. They were full of compassion and kindness on the part of both women. Anandibai was a teenager and Theodocia an older woman. They lived far apart in different parts of the world with huge differences in cultures and customs, and yet they were drawn to each other in various ways. A deep bond was formed between them.

In her letters, Anandibai explained that though Indian women were under the control of their husbands, her life was different. She wrote about everything unabashedly, happy to find someone who would read her every word with interest and treat them as precious. Vignettes from the ordinary lives of Indian households—clothes (sarees, dhotars, angarkhas), eating habits according to caste, eating of betel nuts and leaves, brushing teeth were described. She also mentioned the complex caste system in India, women's silent suffering, about widows and so on. They exchanged newspapers, magazines, flowers, seeds and photographs. She sent *tilgul* (sesame seeds coated with jaggery or sugar) to Theodocia.

Theodocia looked in great amazement at

Anandibai's photograph when she received it. What was that near her nose? Was it a blemish due to an accident or a birthmark? Anandi clarified that it was a nose-ring: 'It consists of one gold wire, upon which are fastened pearls, some pendant and others fixed and star-shaped. We are fond of many ornaments... Holes are bored through the lower part of the left nostril for the nose-ring, and all around the edge of the ear for jewels. This may appear barbarous to the foreign eye; but to us it is a beauty! Everything changes with the clime.'

Anandi's early marriage and motherhood had left its mark on her. She was now frail and fell sick often. This was one of her main reasons to aspire to be a doctor. Her own experiences made her understand the plight of all Indian women.

After being bedridden for almost three weeks, she wrote from Bhuj on 1 November 1880:

This sickness confirms me in my desire to study medicine. Though my sickness was not of a serious nature, yet I was at one time so much affected that I had passed some days and nights without the least relief until we had recourse to professional medical advice and treatment.

Anandibai goes on to say that Indian women keep suffering from various diseases that often start with minor ailments. Women generally hide their illnesses from men, and hesitate to consult male doctors. Therefore, most of the time the illness takes a serious turn and women die. The men, too, are rather careless about such issues concerning women. She felt the need for Indian women medical professionals who could provide their services to sick women and prevent many deaths.

Anandibai was frustrated at the lack of opportunities for those like her who were keen to study to become doctors. Not only were there lack of opportunities for women, it was also a time when Indians were having a tough time accepting modern Western medicine.

Throughout the 18th and 19th centuries, modern medicine was not popular among Indians.

However, with a view to treat Europeans in British India, the British government formed the Indian Medical Service in 1764. Medical training and teaching in local languages started after that. In 1822, the Native Medical Institution was formed and later a committee formed by William Bentinck mentioned the need for a new medical college. This was formed in 1835, known as the Medical College Calcutta. It was the first medical college in India, meant to train Indians as doctors.

Doctors who graduated from here included Umacharan Seth, Rajkrishna De, Dwarkanath Gupta, among others. The first batch of students graduated in October 1838.

Women had a tough time enrolling in these institutions. Many fought against this bias. Finally, on 29 June 1883, Kadambini Basu Ganguly became the first woman to enrol in Calcutta Medical College, a first also in India. Eventually, in 1886, she became the first woman to get a medical degree in Western medicine in India. From 1884, the government began to offer scholarships of Rs 20 per month to all women students. Bidhumukhi Basu and Virginia Mitter were the other early women medical graduates in India.

Around this time, medical colleges and schools were opened in a number of Indian cities including Bombay, Madras and Lahore. In the later part of the nineteenth century, two funds were started to encourage women in medical studies: the Medical Women for India Fund and the Countess of Dufferin Fund. The Dufferin Fund helped open hospitals for women's treatment across India. Eventually, colleges for medical studies for women opened, including Christian Medical College, Vellore, Lady Hardinge Medical College, Delhi, and so on.

Anandibai was among the first Indian women to explore the possibilities of studying medicine, but realized that she was going to meet with resistance in the country.

To Theodocia, she wrote about the lack of opportunities for medical studies in India for women and explained that she looked at the West for women's emancipation. In her letters to her American friend, she began to seriously explore the possibility of travelling to the US to study medicine. She enquired about expenses and told Theodocia that she wanted to stick to Indian food and clothing during her stay there.

The subject of women's suffering featured often in their letters. Anandi wrote about Indian widows.

She also wrote about women's independence: 'When I think over the sufferings of women in India...I am impatient to see the Western light dawn as the harbinger of emancipation...No man or woman should depend upon another for maintenance and necessaries.' Only then, Anandi believed, would there be an end to clashes within the family between women and men.

After receiving Theodocia's photograph, she wrote about her wish to call her 'Aunt'. 'There is a saying among us, "it does not matter much if a mother dies, but let not an aunt die",' she wrote.

The letters—receiving and writing them—infused a fresh lease of life in Anandibai. She now had a friend to turn to, someone who seemed to appreciate and value her. Her days seemed brighter and better.

Chapter Four

Gopalrao was transferred to Calcutta (now Kolkata) in April 1881. The city posed an entirely new challenge for the Joshees. It was far from their home in Maharashtra. The couple found it tough to fit into its culture. Here, too, people stared at them during their evening walks.

The hot and humid weather affected Anandibai's health and she got boils on her face. What a strange place, thought Anandi, looking at the Bengali babus and hearing their inquisitive questions directed at her. How can they ask such rude questions to strangers! Anandibai found Calcutta more troublesome that Bombay.

One evening, Anandibai and Gopalrao were walking in the Esplanade area of Calcutta. A police sepoy came near them. 'Excuse me, sir,' he hailed Gopalrao from a distance.

They stopped. 'Yes?' Gopalrao asked the sepoy.

'Who is this woman with you?' the sepoy inquired.

'What is this about?' Gopalrao asked.

'Please answer my question. Who is this woman with you?' the sepoy repeated.

'She is my wife. Why do you ask?' said Gopalrao.

The sepoy smirked. Within moments it was clear that the sepoy was like everyone else—a curious onlooker—but had taken advantage of his position to ask them this question. Gopalrao lost his cool.

'Tell me your name and I shall report you to the Commissioner,' Gopalrao said, clearly flustered.

The police sepoy sensed trouble. 'Kindly ignore the matter, sir. I hope you enjoy your evening...' and bowing before them the sepoy left immediately.

Their evening was spoiled already. Gopalrao sighed. Anandibai said: 'Either this country is not good for us, or we are doing something that goes against the customs here.'

It was hard to be comfortable even in their living quarters. When Anandibai and Gopalrao read out to each other, their German landlady

said that they quarrelled all night which kept her children and the other tenants up. Anandi got fever and headaches regularly.

Then more trouble came their way. Gopalrao accidentally lost a special dispatch from the Viceroy to the Governor of Bengal and got suspended. Such stressful situations made them want to move to America. The trouble, however, blew over and he got reinstated.

In Calcutta, Anandibai was offered a job in the postal department with a salary of Rs 30 per month. But Anandibai turned it down as she did not want to bow down before the British, who were ruling over India.

The funds for their travel to the US could not be arranged yet. Theodocia offered to help, but Anandibai wanted to be qualified to travel,

and was thus studying hard. Though Calcutta was largely disappointing for the Joshees, they met Raosaheb Dandekar, another Chitpavan Brahmin from Maharashtra. The two families formed a close friendship within a short time. Anandi even lived with them for two months in their Burrabazar home when she was unwell.

Gopalrao was next transferred to Barrackpore, about 25 km north of Calcutta. Within a few months, he was transferred to Serampore, about 30 km from Calcutta. This was a former Danish town on the bank of River Hooghly.

Anandi's experiences in Bombay and Calcutta continued to be repeated in Serampore. Whenever she stepped out of home, people looked at her with wonder and suspicion. She now desperately wanted to be in a place where

people would accept her. She didn't mind if she stood out. But it ought to be because of her talent and success.

Initially, Anandi and Gopalrao wanted to go to the US together. But Gopalrao's two years' leave application was turned down and they realized he could not quit his job. His mother and siblings were dependent on him. Finally, they decided that Anandibai would travel alone to the US. It was a daring decision—maybe even crazy by some measure. But both were brave enough to do something so unusual.

On 12 August 1882, Anandi wrote to Theodocia: 'Considering the future prospects of my life as a physician I must make up my mind to be separated from my husband...I fear no miseries. I shrink not at the recollection of dangers, nor do I fear them. Whatever will be, there will be Heaven for me. I am sure God has created many high souls, like you, who will not neglect me...Everyone must not ride on another's shoulder but walk on his own feet. Perhaps my husband will follow me some time after, but I must not wait for him, as time is so precious.'

People were appalled and outraged when they heard that Mrs Anandibai Joshee was to travel to the United States all by herself. What would she eat? What would she wear in a foreign land? How would she live without her husband? These questions and more, came her way.

Anandibai was going to be in a ship for weeks. She would live in a foreign land for three years studying medicine! It was outrageous, fantastical and impossible! Both Anandibai and Gopalrao's families were strictly against such a move. They felt it was unacceptable, and wondered if Gopalrao was forcing Anandi to run after such absurd ideas, when they should be happy in their own country, concentrating on family matters. It was a mix of tremendous happiness and extreme low for the Joshees at the same time. It was as if everyone in their country had gone against them.

Chapter Five

To travel abroad in nineteenth century India was an almost impossible dream. There were numerous social strictures against it. Most people hesitated to cross the seas to go to a foreign land. There were some who went though, like Abu Talib, an administrator-poet from Awadh. Indian women had travelled abroad earlier, but mostly as labourers or ayahs (maids), in search of work, out of compulsion.

Towards the end of the nineteenth century, Indians began to travel for higher education.

But it wasn't easy to break the taboo, and so Anandibai Joshee's move was pathbreaking.

People began to gather outside the Joshee home in Serampore. Anandibai and Gopalrao could not escape their wrath. 'For how long can we take the flurry of abuses and questioning?' asked Anandi. Gopalrao thought hard. He came upon an idea: he would publicly defend her decision. But Anandibai wanted to do it herself.

'If their queries are answered, perhaps there will be less antagonism,' Gopalrao said. Anandibai wasn't sure, but knew that an explanation was becoming necessary. On 24 February 1883,

Anandibai spoke at Serampore College on 'Why do I go to America?' She answered six questions that people were most curious about. She did so with unusual calm and composure.

Why do I go to America?

I go to America because I wish to study medicine...

Ladies both European and Native are naturally averse to expose themselves in cases of emergency to treatment by doctors of the other sex. There are some female doctors in India from Europe and America, who being foreigners and different in manners, customs and language, have not been of such use to our women as they might. As it is very natural that

Hindu ladies who love their own country and people should not feel at home with the natives of other countries, we Indian women absolutely derive no benefit from these foreign ladies...In my humble opinion, there is a growing need for Hindu lady doctors in India, and I volunteer to qualify myself for one.

Are there no means to study in India?

No. I do not mean to say there are *no* means, but the difficulties are many and great. There is one College at Madras, and midwifery classes are opened in all the Presidencies; but the education imparted is defective and not sufficient, as the instructors who teach the classes are conservative, and to some extent jealous. I do not find fault with them. That is the characteristic of the male sex. We must put up with this inconvenience until we have a class of educated ladies to relieve these men.[...]

I place these unpleasant things before you, that those whom they concern most may rectify them, and those who have never thought of the difficulties may see that I am not going to America through any whim or caprice.

Why do I go alone?

It was at first the intention of my husband and myself to go together, but we were forced to abandon this thought. We have not sufficient funds. [She also explained about her husband's responsibilities towards his family.]

Shall I not be excommunicated when I return to India?

Do you think I should be filled with consternation at this threat? I do not fear it in the least...I propose to myself to make no change in my customs and manners, food or dress...If my countrymen wish to excommunicate me, why do they not do it now?...I have come to Bengal and to a place where there is not a single Maharashtrian. Nobody here knows whether I behave according to my customs and manners, or not. Let us therefore cease to consider what may never happen, and what, when it may happen, will defy human speculation.

What will I do if misfortune befalls me?

[...] A man or a woman who *wishes to act* does not

look at that dark side which others easily foresee. On necessary and inevitable evils which crush him or her to dust, all dispute is vain. When they happen, they must be endured, but it is evident they are oftener dreaded than experienced. [...] To go to foreign countries is not bad, but in some respects better than to stay in one place.... In going to foreign countries, we may enlarge our comprehension, perfect our knowledge, or recover lost arts. Everyone must do what he thinks right...

Why I should do what is not done by any of my sex?

[...] It is enough that the good of one must be the good of all. If anything seems best for all mankind, each one of us must try to bring it about...I am surprised to hear that I should not do this, because it has not been done by others. [...] To desist from duty because we fear failure or suffering is not just. *We must try*. Never mind whether we are victors or victims...The greater the difficulty, the greater our courage...

Chapter Six

There was pin-drop silence as Anandibai Joshee spoke. It was a historic moment, though people sitting there were perhaps not aware of it. She spoke gently but firmly about the disparity between women and men. Her words were so powerful that no one knew how to disagree with them.

The event was reported in the *Theosophist* (April 1883), as 'A Mahratta Lady's Address'. It reported:

> *...she is very likely to become one of the earliest pioneers in one of the grandest and most needed reforms in India, that of female education and the enfranchisement of woman.*

The lecture had a huge impact. H.E.M. James, Director of the General Post Office of India later told Gopalrao: 'I was very glad to hear that Mrs Joshee has made her debut, and has succeeded. Pray give her my congratulations. I wish her every success. In recognition of her courage and public spirit, permit me to offer the enclosed cheque for one hundred rupees which may be useful to her.' Many others wrote congratulating her.

Now that she had the money, travelling to the United States and living there for some time would not be very tough. Anandi asked Theodocia for help finding a place to stay in America. She was still looking for people to travel with.

Before Anandibai's public lecture, Anna Thoburn, a former student of the Woman's Medical College of Pennsylvania (WMCP) had written a letter to the Dean Dr Rachel Bodley in November 1882 on her behalf. She wrote that Anandibai would be a 'real curiosity', 'the first Hindoo woman who has ever set foot on American soil', stating that she was bright and wrote English well.

Anandibai wanted to go to WMCP. To Theodocia, she wrote on 3 April 1883: 'Aunt, rest assured that we will meet very soon.'

The Woman's Medical College of Pennsylvania was founded in 1850 as Female Medical College of Pennsylvania. It was the first medical school in the world to award women the degree of MD. It was formed by some Quakers, and eight women graduated in its first year in 1851, Ann Preston being one of them. To provide clinical experience to the graduates, a group of women founded the Woman's Hospital of Philadelphia in 1861. This became essential as the women graduates were denied access to other hospitals for training. Important early women graduates from WMCP include Mary Putnam Jacobi, an American woman, Clara Swain, the first woman medical missionary who travelled to India in 1869, Anna Broomall, a teacher of obstetrics, Catherina Macfarlane who conducted the first study in preventing pelvic cancers. Others include Susan LaFlesche Pictotte, the first Native American woman doctor, women MDs from China, Syria, South America, and so on.

In 1969, due to financial pressures, the college decided to admit male students and changed its name to Medical College of Pennsylvania. In 1995, it merged with Hahnemann University's medical school and was established as Drexel University College of Medicine in 2002.

Anandibai sailed from Calcutta on the morning of 7 April 1883. Gopalrao sent a letter to Benjamin F. Carpenter (Theodocia's husband) updating the family about Anandibai's journey. During the fifty-nine days of her journey, Anandibai wrote letters to Gopalrao, read books, and quietly observed the sights and sounds aboard the ship.

She was full of wonder and excitement, and not at all afraid about doing this unusual journey.

Her journey was filled with many wonders. She saw people from many parts of the world. Perhaps she was one of the first women from India to do so! There were Africans, Egyptians, people selling exotic fruits, clothes, jewellery, etc.

There were a number of halts during the journey. Anandibai was conscious that she appeared 'different' from others. She was accompanied by some European missionary women, but mostly she kept to herself. She felt uncomfortable going outside at the places the steamer halted, wondering whether people would laugh at her clothes, or take her for an 'ayah', a poor working class woman. But this was just the beginning of her long journey, and gradually she would become more comfortable with her surroundings and confident about herself.

Anandi kept to herself, reading with great relish the books that she carried. She could hardly eat as most of the food aboard was non-vegetarian.

Anandibai reached the United States on 4 June 1883. Theodocia was at the New York Harbour, waiting for her to arrive. No doubt she was eager to finally meet the woman with whom she had been corresponding for so long. The moment arrived that Anandi and Theodocia would cherish for the rest of their lives. They looked at each other with great wonder and affection, hugged and kissed one another. Theodocia treated her guest gently and with a lot of care, ensuring Anandi felt the warmth of the welcome. She took her home and showed her the room where she would stay.

Over the next few days, as the news of her arrival spread, neighbours and friends of the Carpenters rushed to greet Anandibai, the wonder woman who had come all the way from India. Their daughters Helena and Eighmie gave Anandi support and strength. Sitting in a rocking chair with flowers in hand, Anandibai felt like a princess as the women embraced and kissed her and gave her more flowers. She was surrounded by warmth and kindness. Such was the rush of curious neighbours and friends, that Theodocia was eventually forced to shut the windows to give her guest some privacy.

Anandibai's arrival to the United States was even reported with her photograph in *Frank Leslie's Illustrated Newspaper*. Many other publications followed suit. 'The step she takes is significant of the times, shows the breaking down of deep-seated prejudices, and is of peculiar importance,' read one newspaper report, titled 'The First Woman Medical Student From India', written by Mrs J.T. Gracey.

Anandibai missed Gopalrao, but she was also completely at ease in the Carpenters' home and enjoyed the attention and love showered on her. She adored the two children, especially developing a deep attachment with Eighmie.

'Would you like to eat the food that I cook for myself?' she asked Theodocia.

'Of course!' she said. The entire Carpenter family ate the Indian preparations with great relish. They embraced her food, culture and language with enthusiasm. In the morning, everyone would say 'Namaskar' instead of 'Good morning'.

Anandi found her own unique ways to make the Carpenter family her very own. She gave them Marathi names. 'Helena, let me call you Tara,' she said. 'And let Eighmie be Premala.'

'What will you call me? I am your aunt!' said Theodocia, her eyes twinkling with mischief.

'You are my Mavshi [Marathi for Aunt],' said Anandi, giving her a tight hug.

After attending a banquet one day, Anandi had an idea. 'Why don't I organize an Indian banquet?' she asked Theodocia. 'What a great idea!' she said.

The plan was executed to perfection after a few days and with a lot of hard work. The Carpenters' home looked delightfully different. Places were set on the floor with rangoli designs, and flowers and perfumes were showered on the guests. Rice, lentils, vegetables, puran poli, ladoos, vadis, mango preserve, mashed banana with sweetened milk were served. The women wore sarees that Anandibai had taken with her. After chanting of prayers, Anandibai showed them 'how to eat like a Hindu'. (Preparing a morsel with one's fingers and carefully popping it inside the mouth and not dropping it in.)

The American hosts became Anandibai's guests and witnessed how stunning Maharashtrian homes looked during celebrations.

By early September 1883, Anandibai began preparing to enrol into college. She stitched long-sleeved blouses, quilts, nightdresses and aprons for cooking and surgery classes. But which college would she go to? There were several options now.

Chapter Seven

Around the same time, some other women in India were also trying to become doctors, but met with stiff resistance. One such woman was Kadambini Bose Ganguly.

Kadambini Ganguly (Bose) was born in Bhagalpur in 1861, in a progressive family. She was admitted to Banga Mahila Vidyalaya that later merged with Bethune School, Calcutta. At that time, girls were not encouraged to get formal education, especially higher education in sciences. In 1879, Bethune College, which was the first women's college in India, started its classes with one student—Kadambini—who was in the First Year Arts. Soon, another girl, Chandramukhi Bose, joined her in 1881. She had completed her First Year Arts from the Free Church Normal School. The duo got scholarships and passed their BA examination from Bethune College in 1883, becoming the first women graduates of Calcutta University and in India. Kadambini married Dwarkanath Ganguly, her teacher at Bethune College. When she wanted to enrol for a medical course, Calcutta Medical College denied her admission. But she and Dwarkanath fought for it and she was eventually allowed to enrol in 1883. Kadambini, in 1886, became the first Indian woman to graduate in Western medicine in India. It was the same year in which Anandibai Joshee became the first Indian woman to graduate abroad in Western medicine.

Not only in India, women in the West too had to struggle for years to pursue higher studies, especially medicine. The Female Medical College of Pennsylvania was established in 1850 to train women as physicians. It was the first college in

the world to offer women the doctor of medicine degree. The college's first woman dean was Dr Ann Preston, who was also one of the first graduates from the college.

Ann Preston was a doctor and activist in Philadelphia. Born in 1813 in West Grove, Pennsylvania near Philadelphia, she wanted to be a doctor as a young student, but struggled for years against the system due to lack of opportunities for women. After being refused admission in all four Philadelphia medical colleges because she was a woman, Ann Preston attended the newly opened Woman's Medical College of Pennsylvania (WMCP), graduating in its first class in 1851. She was thirty-eight years old then. In 1853, she became professor of physiology and hygiene at the medical college.

Later, when the Philadelphia Medical Society banned women physicians from the city's medical clinics and societies, Preston raised funds for opening a hospital attached to the Women's Medical College. This would help the women who qualified as medical professionals get first-hand experience. She also opened a school of nursing. She became the first woman Dean of the WMCP.

Preparations had started for Anandibai to finalize which college she would go to, and for this, Theodocia wrote to WMCP's Dean Rachel Bodley on 18 June 1883:

Dear Madam,
I have in my care Mrs Anandibai Joshee, a Hindoo lady of high caste. She has come to America to study medicine that she might serve her fellow country women in the

capacity of surgeon and physician. Hearing from many sources that the Female College of Pennsylvania is the best and most thorough in its main points and believing from some things I have heard and seen in print that steps have already been taken to secure for my ward the advantages of your College, I write to ask you to please inform me what arrangements, if any, have been made.

Dean Rachel Bodley wrote to Alfred Jones, Secretary of the College's Executive Committee, seeking a scholarship for Anandibai. Later, Anandibai herself wrote to Jones, explaining her keen interest in studying medicine, her lack of means and what she had studied so far.

WMCP had been providing opportunities to women from various underprivileged backgrounds and Anandibai had knocked on the right door. Rebecca Cole, the second African American woman to receive a medical degree in the United States, had graduated from here in 1867.

Rebecca J. Cole was the second woman African American doctor in the United States. She graduated from the Woman's Medical College of Pennsylvania in 1867. Born in 1846, she became an advocate for the poor and for women's progress and education especially in legal and medical services. She practiced medicine in South Carolina, North Carolina, Washington D.C. and Philadelphia.

Sociologist W.E.B. DuBois in an 1899 study had argued that African Americans were dying of consumption due to their poor hygiene practices. Cole accused DuBois that the data collected for the study had been erroneous. She argued that the high African American mortality rates were due to the refusal of white doctors to collect comprehensive medical histories of their black patients. She won a case when she refused to form a separate group for coloured women in the Ladies' Centennial Committee of Philadelphia that was planning the hundredth anniversary of the Declaration of Independence.

A British woman from India and a Russian woman had also applied around the same time as Anandibai, to the WMCP. The college offered Anandibai a place to stay and a scholarship for the three-year course.

Meanwhile, though Anandibai was keen on enrolling in WMCP even before she had reached the US, she wanted to explore other possibilities. The Homeopathic College at New York and the medical college at Boston were also trying to woo her. Both institutions made similar offers to her, but eventually Anandibai chose the Philadelphia college.

Anandibai reached Philadelphia on September 28, accompanied by Mrs Carpenter. Anandibai and Theodocia went to meet Dr Rachel Bodley. As Anandi entered the Dean's room, the Dean was bowled over by this young woman full of conviction and simplicity. Bodley kissed her on the cheek, absolutely delighted that she had come all the way from India to study medicine in her institution.

Dr Bodley organized a reception for her new student. It was attended by a few hundred people, who came to congratulate her and 'see' for themselves what this slight-looking Indian woman with so much courage looked like. Wearing a red pitambar, she stood along with Bodley and Theodocia to welcome the guests. The event was reported in the local papers as well as in the *Mahratta* and the *Theosophist* in India. In America Anandibai Joshee became a star attraction for her unusual journey, and her enthusiasm, merit and grit.

She passed her Matriculation or entrance examination to the college on 3 October 1883, and became a student of the WMCP.

Now a strange mix of feelings swept over

Anandi. She was going to start a new phase of her life. This time, it all depended on her. She was in charge.

Chapter Eight

Anandibai Joshee had always been hardworking. Few could match her physical and mental strength. But now the path was new and she had much to learn. Classes started in October. She had set up her own space with a lot of enthusiasm and once the classes began, she cooked and cleaned, bathed, ate, and left for college. On returning to her room, she studied, wrote letters, ate, and slept like a log.

She met many women, all of whom had struggled in their own ways to be able to study medicine. There was Koi Okami from Japan, Sabat M. Islambooly from Syria. There was an English woman from India and another from Russia. The different batches of medical students interacted from time to time. Bit by bit, they got to know each other and their stories of struggle to have come this far. Even at WMCP, Anandibai was the centre of attention. Though she was not the first international student there, she had travelled far from India to get there. It seemed almost unbelievable that this woman could be bold enough to overcome so many odds to achieve her dreams.

Though Anandi continued to eat simple meals cooked by herself, the weather began to change in America, prompting her to change the way she wore her saree. The Maharashtrian style of draping exposed the legs a bit and she felt very cold, so she changed the draping pattern into the Gujarati style, and wore stockings, covered shoes, a warm blouse and a shawl. It was, she felt, another Indian style of draping the saree so she would be keeping her promise of sticking to Indian culture and customs during her stay here. She covered her head with the free end of the saree. Bangles jingling in her hands, bindi on her forehead, mangalsutra in place, she was ready to attend classes.

It would be intense three years of studies, after which, once she got her medical degree, she would spend a year in a hospital for practical training before setting off for India. Her dream was to return to India with a medical degree and to begin treating patients.

What respect she would earn! What blessings she would be showered with! How many sick people she would cure! People would love her and her name would go down in history!

Anandibai was then receiving the James Fund, initiated by H.E.M. James, the Director General of the Post Offices of India. After he gave a sum of rupees one hundred to pay for Anandibai's travel to the United States and for her education, he continued the effort even later. He wrote a circular, published in Calcutta newspapers, about her efforts to study medicine in the US, and after that British officials from the Viceroy and Governor-General to the Chief Justice of Bengal contributed to this fund.

The college schedule was gruelling and as winter set in, cooking every day got tougher.

The smoke bellowed from the stove causing terrible coughs and breathing trouble. So much of household work along with studies exhausted Anandi. By the end of the month, Bodley had to take a call. 'Move in to my place,' she said. Anandi was glad to be offered a place with people around her, and things improved. She was bright and hardworking and did very well in her examination. The weeks were brutally busy with back-to-back lectures and standing continuously for hours. But she enjoyed every bit of it!

~

People around her took a lot of interest in her, and that delighted Anandibai. In September 1883, before leaving for Philadelphia, she wrote down her 'mental photograph' in Theodocia's diary. As

Anandi worked hard in her medical studies, back in Roselle, Theodocia leafed through the pages, missing her dear niece sorely.

In it, Anandi wrote about her favourite things: white was her favourite colour, mango her favourite tree; she loved mountains, sunrise, sunset, the scent of jasmine, the shine of diamond, the sound of violin and lyre, among other things. She loved the Taj Mahal, poets Manu, Pope and Kalidasa, Muktabai and Janabai, and her favourite text was the Bhagvat Gita.

Here is what some pages from the notebook contained:

Where would you prefer to live?

In Roselle now, hereafter in Heaven.

What is your favourite amusement?

Reading

What is your favourite trait of character?

Sincerity

What trait do you most detest?

Dishonesty and infidelity

If not yourself, whom would you like to be?

No one

What are the sweetest words?

Love, charity, truth and hope

What is your aim?

To be useful.

What is your motto?

The Lord will provide.

Meanwhile, in Philadelphia, Anandi enjoyed the first snowfall. The ground was covered with a thick white layer. Sometimes it rained making the paths dirty and slippery. Walking was a risky business especially for Anandi and all the medical students who came from warmer regions. Anandi wrote letters home describing all of this.

During the holidays, she enjoyed herself thoroughly with Theodocia and the rest of the Carpenters, playing with snowballs and 'sleigh' rides. However, the brutal weather and the gruelling class schedule took a toll on her health. Or perhaps it was something else. Maybe her recurrent weakness and illnesses had something to do with bearing a child at such a young age. Sometimes she had spells of cold, fever, chills and wondered if it was due to fatigue.

Initially, Anandi had asked Gopalrao to join her and the fare could be arranged by selling her jewellery. However, the longer she stayed in the United States, studies took up most of her time. She got used to being without him by her side constantly.

Anandi advised Gopalrao to postpone his visit so he could join her when she passed her final examination and joined a hospital. If he scheduled his visit then, they could return to India together.

Anandibai was diagnosed with diphtheria, and she was restricted to bed for weeks. Being far from home, Anandi was moved by the kindness of strangers. How poorly she had often been treated by her mother and husband! And here, in America, people were so caring though they hardly knew her. Her classmates sent her fruits, letters and flowers.

During her years as a medical student, Anandibai faced many situations that she handled with patience and calm, showing what an outstanding medical professional she would make.

In 1884, she was in a surgery class assisting in a post-mortem dissection performed by a senior.

After the dissection session was over, the professor and students left, and only Anandibai was in the room, when a woman, clearly of unsound mind, entered. There were many sharp instruments like scalpels, knives, scissors lying around, and the woman started asking Anandi repeatedly what she was doing there. Realizing the danger, Anandi remained calm and edged towards the door. Luckily, an attendant came to take the woman, who had escaped from her confined treatment area.

At the Morristown Insane Asylum, something similar took place, and here too Anandi was unusually calm. A woman wanted to shake hands with her and hugged her so tight she was breathless and suffocated. She freed herself from the clasp by drawing away her attention with kind words. Anandi was always understanding and sensitive and already there were indications what a patient and impressive doctor she was going to be.

She never dithered from her conviction to return to India. Never for once did she forget the reason she had travelled to the US—to learn so that she could be back in her country to serve women in need. When Gopalrao suggested they shift base to America, Anandi wrote that she would want to be back in India and be useful to her 'fellow creatures'.

Chapter Nine

In her letters to Gopalrao, Anandibai's strong personality began to emerge now. She continued to be the devoted wife, but she was also independent, hardworking and confident, and expressed herself clearly and firmly.

Once, Gopalrao took offence on seeing a photograph in which the loose end of Anandi's saree was not exactly in place. He wrote to her harshly.

Anandibai was devastated. But she was firm this time. She reminded him that once Gopalrao himself had asked her to dress like a Western woman if the weather demanded it, and to even eat meat if it was necessary. In any case, she had not done any of these, and had stuck to her way of life as she had promised. Moreover, the loose end of her saree had moved a bit purely by accident, and no one had noticed it, neither she, nor the photographer, or anyone else around.

This was a new aspect to her personality, in which she spoke up without any fear or inhibition, not afraid to disagree with Gopalrao.

'It is sad that we do not share the same views these days,' she tells Gopalrao. There is a new firmness in her voice.

After all those years of being physically abused by her husband, Anandibai was now in control of her life. She had been offered scholarships to study, her personality and talent had been appreciated, and she was able to work hard and do well in her work, and most importantly, she found freedom. All those people in the United States glad to give her the opportunity to study in their institutions, offering her stay and scholarship were impressed by her dedication. All this wiped away her fears and sorrows and infused in her a new confidence.

Anandibai's life is proof that even after facing harsh abuse, it is possible to find happiness. The time had now come to answer her abuser with calm and strength.

> *It is very difficult to decide whether your treatment of me was good or bad. If you ask me, I would answer that it was both. It seems to have been right in view of its ultimate goal;*

but, in all fairness, one is compelled to admit that it was wrong, considering its possible effects on a child's mind.

Anandibai wrote how she was beaten up mercilessly by blocks of wood or had chairs thrown at her when she was just a child, too young to realize what marriage was or how she would benefit from studying. The beatings had scarred her, and his threats to leave her had made her afraid, she said. These things had affected her young mind, but she had been taught to always show patience. But now, after all these years, she had moved to a new place where she felt much happier. She could leave those traumatic moments in a distant past.

~

In June 1884, Gopalrao started his travel to the United States. Anandi meanwhile continued with her studies, which were tough and demanded a lot of time. She was a sincere student, who planned meticulously. Sometimes her schedule continued for fifteen to sixteen hours but she enjoyed every bit of it.

Gopalrao reached California in spring 1885. Now that he was so near to where she was, Anandibai kept wondering when they should meet eventually, and when that happened after so long, how would they greet each other.

Gopalrao finally reached Roselle where they met after so long. After a few months there, the Joshees and the Carpenters travelled to various parts of the US. When college reopened in

October 1884, Anandibai returned to her studies, perhaps a bit embarrassed that her husband had quit his job.

Chapter Ten

Anandibai Joshee had joined medical classes in October 1883. The course was to be completed in three years and then she would stay on for another year for practical training. After October 1885, she submitted her thesis on 'Obstetrics among the Aryan Hindoos' for the Doctor of Medicine degree. Obstetrics is the branch of medicine and surgery that deals with childbirth and the assistance required for it, including midwifery.

In her thesis, Anandi mentioned the long history and tradition of Indian medical science. Obstetrics deserved careful study and its traditional history and practices should not be ignored, she wrote. She detailed the skill of traditional doctors, their learning often ignored by Western medical professionals. In her work, she attempted to underline the significance and importance of Indian traditional medicine, and its usefulness.

Anandibai was now in the final leg of her course, busy preparing for her final exams in March 1886, which would be followed by internship. She got an offer of a special six-month internship from the New England Hospital for Women and Children at Boston from May. For this, she cancelled her summer vacation with the Carpenters. It was indeed a special offer many were not lucky to get.

It was a long examination schedule and Anandi was tired to the bone. On the final day of the final examination, she almost broke down. 'I could not even see whether I finished my sentence. I pinned the papers together and left the room without even bowing to the Professor!' she lamented in a letter to Theodocia.

From India meanwhile, Anandibai had been offered a job on her return as a qualified doctor. The princely state of Kolhapur in the Bombay Presidency had opened the Edward Albert Memorial Hospital. They wanted to open 'a class for female medical pupils', providing them with financial support. A woman doctor would be appointed from abroad to take charge of the ward.

The Dewan of Kolhapur wrote to the WMCP Dean looking for an ideal candidate. Anandibai's name had been recommended by a high official in India. She would be in charge of the Edward Albert Hospital under the general supervision of the State doctor, and train a class of girls who were studying medicine.

Her dream job was offered to her even before she completed her studies! Anandibai was walking on air!

Anandibai Joshee would get a monthly salary of Rs 300, to be increased to Rs 400 after two years, and to Rs 500 after five years. She would get a place to stay and travel fare to reach

Pandita Ramabai was born Ramabai Dongre in 1858. Her father was a Sanskrit scholar who taught her Sanskrit at home. After her parents died, she and her brother travelled across India reciting Sanskrit scriptures and she earned the title of *pandita*, a Sanskrit scholar and *sarasvati*, following an examination by the University of Calcutta.

In 1880, she married Bipin Behari Medhvi, a Bengali lawyer. He died in less than two years after the marriage and Ramabai moved to Pune with her daughter Manorama. She founded the Arya Mahila Samaj, a society to work against child marriage. Her first book, *Morals for Women* (Marathi: *Stri Dharma Niti*) was published. Speaking before the British Hunter Commission on Education in India, Ramabai spoke in favour of women's education, including medical studies. This created a great sensation in the country, and led to the Women's Medical Movement with the Countess of Dufferin Fund, to improve women's healthcare in India.

She travelled to Britain in 1883, hoping to study medicine there. Not unexpectedly, she faced opposition. During this time, she and her daughter converted to Christianity. Ramabai then travelled to the USA in 1886 to attend the graduation ceremony of the Woman's Medical College in Philadelphia where Anandibai Joshee graduated as a doctor. She remained in the US for two years, translating textbooks and giving lectures. She also wrote *The High-Caste Hindu Woman*, a book on the oppression of women in India. She returned to India in 1888 and worked for women's education and emancipation.

After the ceremony, a message arrived from the office of Queen Victoria of England. It was a pathbreaking event in the history of women's emancipation for sure.

Now that Anandibai Joshee had become a doctor and was about to join the internship, she planned several trips across the US with her friends and acquaintances. Pandita Ramabai was also with her along with her daughter Manorama. Anandibai had grown deeply attached to her, and looked after Manorama when she fell ill.

Soon after, Anandibai fell ill too. They reached Roselle, where Gopalrao joined them. During this period, she was constantly ill with brief spells of good health.

Anandibai's next stop was the New England Hospital for her internship. Here, she worked hard as usual. But around the same time–May 1886–her illness resurfaced, and she was quite miserable. She had taken charge of the medical ward, and was frightfully busy all day. But her throat was so sore she could not speak. The illness worsened, confining Anandibai to a room. She turned pale and had to stop working.

She showed some improvement and went on a break with Eighmie to New York in mid-July, where she even enjoyed herself eating strawberries and doing stitching, but the illness seemed to be overpowering her gradually. Her friends got worried, and Anandi cut short the vacation. Fevers and chills came several times a day, apart from body aches. She had to give up her internship due to the illness and to return to Roselle to the Carpenter home.

But she was not afraid, nor did she worry that it could be fatal. She spent her last month in

Roselle mostly confined to bed, down with fever, weakness, body ache and terrible cough.

It was time to return to India.

~

Anandibai's eleven trunks were packed, most of them containing souvenirs from her stay in the United States—the gifts and honours she had received.

Anandi and Gopalrao were to set off on 9 October 1886. Anandi was so frail and vulnerable that even the movement of the carriage was painful for her. The Carpenter family along with Pandita Ramabai came to say goodbye. A bunch of flowers in hand, Anandi leaned on Theodocia's shoulder till they reached the steamer 'Etruria'.

She was happy to lie down, but the

journey back was extremely tough. Her health deteriorated steadily and Gopalrao was helpless as he had no idea how to offer her relief. He kept writing to Theodocia as Anandibai was unable to even sit up and write a few lines. She was seasick with constant coughs. The weather was bad, the sea was rough, there were storms. She cried often, worrying that she would die en route.

When they landed in Bombay on 16 November 1886, after travelling for over a month, Anandibai was in great misery. She was unable to enjoy the moment that she had longed for all these years. Here she was, back in her country as the first woman doctor in India trained in America, her arrival reported in newspapers. Praises were also showered on Gopalrao for the unusual task he had taken up to support his wife to pursue higher studies so she could be of value to the nation.

After their return, her condition worsened, and Gopalrao changed doctors and medical treatments. She was diagnosed with 'consumption'. Doctors suggested that she be shifted to the drier Pune. Gopalrao wanted Anandi to be treated by an ayurvedic Vaidya, but the physician refused to treat her as she had trained as a doctor abroad. Eventually, another doctor agreed to treat her. But her condition kept worsening. Nothing worked. Anandibai could not join her work at Kolhapur as she was too ill.

Dr Anandibai Joshee died on 26 February 1887, about three months after returning to India.

Her ashes were not immersed in a holy river

as is customary in the Hindu tradition. Instead, Gopalrao sent the ashes to America. It was buried by the Carpenters in the cemetery at Poughkeepsie, New York.

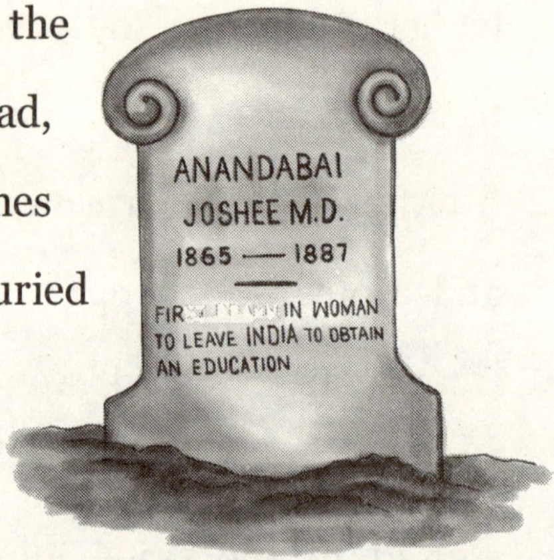

Among the many people Anandibai came to know in the United States, was Caroline Dall. Later, Dall was to write the first biography of Anandibai in 1888. She was an American author and feminist, who knew Anandi for three years. She also greatly admired Pandita Ramabai.

Anandibai Joshee was a trailblazer. Her relationship with her husband was complex, and played an important role in her success. While he taught her to dream big, he was also abusive. It is said that he was ambitious and wanted to create a name for himself as a reformer and thus he moulded Anandi accordingly to suit his purpose. But it is important to note that even if Gopalrao had taught her to dream, Anandi made those dreams her own. It was *her* hard work and *her* success alone.

In the success stories of women, there are often attempts made to give part of the credit to others—especially men—who have inspired, motivated and backed them. But Anandi's words that we can read in her letters and public speeches, indicate that she had a deep understanding on the equality of women and men. She had always been a girl of great conviction and courage, and she found herself truly free when she travelled and lived in a foreign land. She grew mature and her personality changed. She remained loyal to her country and to her partner through all the difficulties she faced.

It is ironic that Anandi died so young, without being able to put to use the valuable knowledge for which she had to go through such hardship! But she was a champion of women's rights, who showed many women how to dream big. She has influenced generations of women into joining the medical profession and is a name to remember when it comes to women's equality.

Anandibai Joshee:
A Timeline

- 31 March 1865: A girl is born in Kalyan region of Bombay Presidency, to Ganpatrao Joshi and Gangabai Joshi. She is named Yamuna.
- 1874: Yamuna is married to Gopalrao Joshee, a widower seventeen years older than her. Her name is changed to Anandi, meaning 'Joy of my heart'.
- March 1880: Theodocia Carpenter, a woman from the United States writes to Anandibai Joshee, after finding out from a publication

about her interest in pursuing higher studies in that country.

- 24 February 1883: Anandibai Joshee speaks in public at Bengal's Serampore College, on 'Why Do I Go to America?"
- 7 April 1883: She sets off from Calcutta for the United States.
- 4 June 1883: Anandibai reaches the US.
- October 1883: She passes her entrance examination and formally enrols as a medical student in the Woman's Medical College of Pennsylvania.
- March 1886: Anandibai Joshee graduates with a Doctor of Medicine (MD) degree from the Woman's Medical College of Pennsylvania, becoming the first woman from India to receive the degree of medicine abroad.

- 1 June 1886: Anandibai is offered a contract as the Physician-in-charge of the Female Wards of the Albert Edwards Hospital, Kolhapur, India.
- 9 October 1886: Anandibai and Gopalrao set off from New York to Bombay.
- 16 November 1886: They reach Bombay.
- 26 February 1887: Dr Anandibai Joshee dies in Pune.

Author's Note

I was truly inspired by Anandibai's life while working on this book.

For my research, I referred to the book *The Life of Dr Anandabai Joshee, A Kinswoman of Pundita Ramabai* by Mrs Caroline Healey Dall (Boston, Robert Brothers, 1888), the Drexel University Libraries online archives for the letters related to Anandibai's life, and *A Fragmented Feminism, The Life and Letters of Anandibai Joshee*, Meera Kosambi (Routledge, London and New York, 2020), among others.

Many articles such as 'Anandibai Joshee: Retrieving A Fragmented Feminist Image', by Meera Kosambi, *Economic & Political Weekly*, 7 December 1996, published in jstor.org as well as philadelphiaencyclopaedia.org, bethunecollege.ac.in, medicalcollege.kolkata.in were my other references.

I also used for my reference information from Kashibai Kanitkar's book *Dr Anandibai Joshi Yanche Charitra Va Patre*, published by Sarita Prakashan, 2019; 'Through a Changing Feminist Lens: Three Biographies of Anandibai Joshi' by Prachi Gurjarpardhye in the *Economic & Political Weekly*, 16 August 2014 (published in jstor.org);, as well as letters and reports on Anandibai published in the *Theosophist* from the archives on theosophy.world/resource/

publications. In addition, I referred to excerpts from *Radical Spirits: India's First Woman Doctor and Her American Champions* by Nandini Patwardhan, Story Artisan Press, 2020, published in thedispatch.in, and *Books, Bangles and Bravado* by Jill Kar, published in Hektoen International (hekint.org).

Thank you Sudeshna Shome Ghosh for asking me to do this series that now has eight books. Thank you Devashish Verma for the fabulous illustrations.

Swati Sengupta

HAVE YOU READ ALL THE *INCREDIBLE LIVES* BOOKS?

The Incredible Life of Milkha Singh: The Runner Who Could Fly

He was an athlete who overcame life's odds to become one of India's greatest sporstpersons. This is his inspiring story of grit and determination.

In a small village in Punjab, little Milkha Singh grew up, loved by his parents, surrounded by open fields where he could run, play, and fly kites. In the heat of summer, when he had to walk to school barefoot, he would run like the wind so he could get home fast. And then, one day, in the midst of terrible violence and upheaval, his family and home were snatched away forever. Milkha, still a teenager, found himself alone and friendless, till he was recruited into the Army. Here, he finally found his passion and joy—running.

The Incredible Life of Jhalkari Bai: The Braveheart Warrior

She was the bravest girl in her village. And one day, she became one of the bravest women her country had ever known.

Jhalkari Bai grew up in Bhojla, many miles away from the city of Jhansi. Far from the grand forts and palaces and illustrious kings and queens of Jhansi, in her village, she was known for her great strength and bravery—fighting off tigers and dacoits all alone. She nurtured a fierce desire to be a soldier, and to do amazing acts of courage. Today, Jhalkari Bai is present as just a footnote in history. But she lives on in the hearts of her people in Jhansi, Bhojla and beyond. This is her incredible and memorable story of bravery and sacrifice.

The Incredible Life of Birsa Munda: The Great Revolutionary

He was a simple Adivasi boy. But one day he had to stand up and protest all the wrongs being done to his people. And so an unforgettable revolutionary was born.

Birsa Munda lived in one of the villages that dotted the Chhotanagpur region in today's Jharkhand. He was a dreamy boy with an uncanny ability to mesmerise not only humans but birds and animals too with his words and music. As he grew up, he became more and more aware of the exploitation of the Adivasi people by rich landowners and the British government. Birsa spoke out one day, and from that moment on, he started a journey that saw him become one of India's greatest tribal leaders and icons of resistance.

The Incredible Life of Savitribai Phule: The Fearless Reformer

All she wanted was to be able to go to school. But she and many like her were denied this because of their caste. That did not stop her.

When she was nine years old, Savitri was married to thirteen-year-old Jyotirao Phule. Savitri yearned to be able to go to school, to read books. Jyotiba wanted his wife to be educated as well, and so he taught her. Soon, she learnt not just to read and write, but also trained as a teacher. Together, Savitribai and Jyotirao Phule started schools where girls and boys, dalit children, and those who had been shunned from schools till then could get educated. They fought against caste atrocities. They made sure that women learnt of their rights to exist with dignity.

The Incredible Life of Bhagat Singh: The Indomitable Freedom Fighter

He had a burning desire to see India as an independent country. He would stop at nothing to make it happen.

Born in 1907 to a family of farmers in Punjab, Bhagat Singh at the age of three had declared that he was sowing guns so he could fight the British colonisers. As he grew up, Bhagat Singh became a widely read and fiercely intelligent man. He would dedicate his life to not only making India free but also towards creating a more equitable society.

The Incredible Life of Arati Saha: The Swimmer Who Wouldn't Give Up

From the moment she learnt to swim, Arati set her eyes on difficult challenges. Then she decided to do what no Asian woman had done before—swim the English Channel.

Arati Saha was born in 1940, and learnt to swim in the Hooghly river in Calcutta as a child. At the age of eight, she competed in the National Championship in Bombay, winning silver and bronze medals. In 1952, she was selected as one of the first four women to represent independent India at the Helsinki Summer Olympics. At eleven years and ten months she was the youngest Indian Olympian—a record that stands till this day. By the time she was eighteen, Arati was looking for a fresh challenge—she decided to swim the English Channel.

The Incredible Life of Satyendranath Bose: A Great Scientist of the World

He was a brilliant child who delighted in playing with numbers. He went on to become one of the greatest scientists of the world, his name joined with Albert Einstein's forever!

A little boy growing up in Calcutta (now Kolkata) is brilliant in mathematics, and has an astonishing capacity to remember anything he has seen just once. In school, he is forever remembered as the only student to score 110 out of 100 in maths! The boy, Satyendranath Bose, would go on to propose theories that would change the field of physics forever.